Social Media Marketing Made Simple

How to get the most out of social media marketing for your business

Nazir Ahmed PMP

Director, Digital Nova Pte Ltd, Singapore
Google Certified Professional

Social Media Marketing Made Simple

How to get the most out of social media marketing for your business

Copyright © 2018 Nazir Ahmed, Digital Nova Pte Ltd, Singapore

Table of Contents

Introduction

There is no doubt that social media is a big place. It is safe to say that it is a replica of our physical world because virtually everything that happens in the physical world now takes place on social media too. People engage each other in conversations in our physical world; people do same on social media. People share business information and ideas in the physical world, the same happens on social media too. We can say that social media is an extension of our physical world.

During the early days of social media, social media platforms were places where people could do basic things like connecting with friends and family and sharing pictures, catching up, etc. But today, social media has evolved more than just a place to share pictures and engage in vanities. Though there are still people, who use social media for the most basic things, a lot of people and businesses are now doing more with social media. People are now increasing exposure for their brands and businesses using social media; people are now connecting with more clients using social media, people are now dishing out marketing contents using social media. In fact, the list is endless. Social media is now the real world while our physical world has turned to be the virtual world.

When people and businesses use social media as a marketing tool for their brands, it is called social media marketing. Social media marketing is the in-thing now, as it has proven to be more and more efficient than traditional marketing. While traditional marketing involves creating and sharing marketing contents on traditional communication media such as newspapers, magazines, television, etc.; social media marketing has to do with creating and sharing marketing content on social media platforms to help command user engagement with the aim of increasing exposure for a business or brand. So, instead of just coming on Facebook or Instagram to post vacation pictures and make posts about your life, you can rather use the platforms to propagate your business. Use them to get more people to be aware of your business.

All the coordinated activities that people do on social media with the sole aim of getting their businesses before people on social media are called social media campaigns. Every day, people set up social media marketing campaigns to achieve various goals. There are many things you must put into consideration before starting any social media marketing campaign. One of these things is the goal of your business. With the goal of your business in mind, you will be able to determine the perfect social media platform and the best strategy that you need to employ for your campaigns. Many times, those who want to run social media marketing campaigns find it really difficult to develop an effective strategy – one that is in line with the goal of their business. And the result is that they create social media marketing campaigns that don't yield the intended result.

The type of business that you run is what determines the strategy you can employ for your social media marketing campaigns. Different businesses need different strategies to be able to run effective social media marketing campaigns. A campaign that does well for a consulting business may not do well for a business that is more into fashion. This is where social media marketing gets tricky and why a lot of people fail to get positive results when they run social media marketing campaigns.

To run an effective social media marketing campaign, you need to understand your business and your business goals as well. They are the things that you need to develop an effective strategy for your campaigns. Like I said earlier, not many people know how to develop a good strategy for their social media marketing campaigns. If you fall into this group, do not worry, by the time you are done reading this book, you would have learned how to develop a good strategy for your social media marketing campaigns. Armed with the required information, creating effective campaigns that yield results will become a walk in the park for you.

Who is this book for?

- Members of marketing team of businesses
- Solopreneurs who want to take their business further through social media marketing

Note: This book is not about how to optimize social media profile neither is it about how to grow your social media following, it is strictly how to develop an effective social media strategy that brings results. Let's get straight to business!

Chapter One: Why bother

A question that people ask all the time is, *"why do I need social media marketing even when traditional marketing is already doing it for me?"*

If you are asking the above question, it means that you are also asking why you need orange juice when you could simply stick to oranges. It means you are asking why you need machines for agriculture instead of sticking to crude farm implements. Yes, there was a time that traditional marketing did it for businesses, but that period is long gone. And that's the truth; so if you must take your business to the next level, you must adopt the current best practices when it comes to marketing. If you doubt why you need social media marketing, then you need to look at the facts below to help you get the motivation you need.

Four strong reasons to consider social media marketing:

1. Social media is where your customers hang out

Every day, millions and millions of people visit social media platforms to connect with friends and family. People always have new gist to share with friends and followers on social media. Like we said before, it is now an extension of the physical world that we live in. Humans are social beings who thrive in the company of others; this explains why there are a lot of people on social media, and every day, new people continue to join. Currently, there are more than 100 million people who use Instagram every month. More than one billion people are active on Facebook. Because of the huge number of people that make join and make use of Facebook every month, Facebook continues to add more and more data centers to their already existing one. What message does all these information send? That more and more activities are taking place on social media.

Because social media is now the "new" real world and by virtual of the fact that we are social beings who thrive in the company of others, we always want to hang out with others; this time around, not in parks, but on social media.

Now, tell me a better way of getting more customers to patronize you than bringing your business to where they are. When you bring your business to where your customers are through social media marketing, you make it easy for them to find and patronize you. You need to know that when people want to make purchases, they always start their search online and from home. After their first search, they spend many days gathering more information about the product or service they need, and this research is always done online. What helps your business to be visible to potential customers when they do researches online in this age is social media marketing.

Imagine what is going to happen to your business if the only channels through which you are creating awareness about it is traditional media? It could be the reason why you are not making sales. If you don't have a way of exposing your business to the huge population on social media, your business does not only suffer, but your reputation suffers too.

Not so many people watch TV commercials anymore, but almost everybody visits one social media platform or the other each day. So, if you don't want to run out of business, you must employ a good social media marketing strategy today. Social media offers you a huge audience to share the message of your brand with. The audience is way more than what any traditional media can offer. Hence, by adopting a good social media marketing strategy, you are placing your business directly before your existing and potential customers. You know what? It is way cheaper.

2. Social media is an important part of how your business gets found online

By the time you understand the huge role that social media marketing plays in making sure that your business is found online, you won't have any doubt in mind regarding employing a social media marketing strategy for your business.

Social media has changed the way we communicate and access information. It has also changed so many of our perceptions. Like we said earlier, the first place that people turn to when they are searching for a product or service is online. And when they get online, they want to read about what other people are saying about the product or service they are looking for. They want to know how long it takes the business to respond to queries and complaints. Social media marketing helps you to always be there to respond to the queries of your existing and potential customers. If you don't have a strong presence on social media, your reputation will suffer greatly. The reason is that once you are not findable, people begin to question your credibility.

Remember that the internet and social media in extension is the first place that people go to when they are searching for new products and services. If you are not active on social media through social media marketing, people won't find you when they are searching for products and services, and what that means is that you will be losing out on the huge population of people who are online.

You stand innumerable risks if people can't find your business on social media. To put it simply, your business will suffer. People always want to hear firsthand information about your business, and social media marketing is one of the best ways you can provide them with this information that they are seeking. Furthermore, when people do searches on Google and the other search engines, social media profiles of businesses related to the searches that the visitor is doing pops up. What does that tell you? Without an efficient social media marketing strategy, you will be losing out on search engine traffic. And you know that search engine traffic means a lot to your business.

3. Social media represents a powerful means of building a strong relationship with customers

One of the aims of social media is to help people build healthy relationships, whether it is a romantic relationship or business relationship. Even though there are other means through which you can reach out to your customers and build a relationship with them, social media just takes the whole relationship building thing to a new level. With social media, you can read reviews about your business, exchange relevant information with your audience, and leverage trusted networks of experts and friends. Even if it is for the sole purpose of building a relationship with your audience, social media marketing is definitely worth it.

Remember that when trying to build a relationship with your customers, relevance is of utmost importance. Let me explain what I mean by relevance in simple words. Imagine that a customer bought your product and wasn't comfortable with what he/she got and proceeded to write a negative review about your product or service; how and when do you respond to clear the issue? Do you respond 6 months after the complaint? Or do you respond swiftly and make moves towards addressing the raised concerns? You see; if you are responding six months after a complaint was made, your response at that time is no longer relevant. Hence, to maintain relevance, your approaches towards building a relationship with your customers should be in real-time.

4. You can target a specific demographic or audience

Imagine that you have put up a promotional content about your business in a local newspaper, would there be a restriction on those who would see the content? The answer is no because a newspaper is for everybody. And by putting up a promotional content about your business for both those who need your business and those who don't need it, you would have wasted a lot of money.

Social media marketing helps you avoid the above scenario by offering you the chance to choose who you want to see your content; this is called audience targeting. Unlike in traditional marketing methods where you roll out your content to everybody out there, social media marketing allows you to target only those who need your business. With social media marketing, you can target specific demographics, age groups, gender, interest, etc. This way, your advertisement or promotional content is only shown to those who want to see it. This helps you save money by not wasting your ad budget or content promotion budget showing your content or ad to those who don't need it.

Traditional advertising does not offer this benefit, you just reel out generic content and expect that the right audience gets to see it, which results in a lot of loss. Besides ensuring that only the right audience gets to see your content, the audience targeting that social media marketing offers helps you to A/B test your campaigns against several metrics. After targeting a particular demographic with no good result, you can always target other demographics until you hit the right metrics, that's an advantage that social media marketing offers.

The four reasons above are enough to make you bother with social media marketing. You have seen that social media is where your customers are, and you must take your business to them where they are, next you need to learn how to develop an effective strategy for your social media marketing campaigns.

Chapter Two: Start with a plan

If you want to build a house, what do you start with? You start with a house plan. You meet an architect and lay out your goals to him and he, in turn, helps you to draw a building plan that captures your goals. The building plan that the architect draws for you captures everything that the house you want to build would contain. It would capture where there would be fixtures, and where there would be open spaces. And without the plan, building the house would be so difficult because the building would be going in circles.

The same way you need a plan to build a house, that's the same way you need a plan to start a business and the same way you need a plan to run an effective social media marketing campaign. The mistake that most people make is that they usually wake up and tumble into social media marketing. They don't understand that social media marketing is serious business and must be taken seriously if one wants to see results. Social media marketing is different from just sharing vacation photos on

Instagram; it goes way beyond that. You need a plan to run an effective social media marketing campaign.

The plan we are talking about is like your business plan. It is not just something you hurry over. You have to document every step you need to run your campaign. You are 538% more likely to report success if you document your social media marketing plan. This is the same way you are 100% more likely to succeed in business if you have a good business plan. The bottom line is that you need a documented strategy that is focused on your goals if you want to see results with your social media marketing.

Now, planning their social media strategy is where most get it wrong in their social media marketing. But once you have been able to develop a good strategy, then you have already done half of your work. In this chapter, we'll take an in-depth look at how to create a good social media marketing strategy that delivers results.

What is social media strategy?

We talked about a building plan and noted that it is needed when you want to build a house. Now, for your social media marketing, what you need is a social media strategy. So we can say that a social media strategy is to social media marketing what architectural design is to a house. Your social media strategy captures everything concerning how you will plan, run, and measure all your activities as regards social media marketing. You can create a social media strategy in three easy steps, and we are going to talk about these steps shortly, but before then, let's quickly look at the tools you need to plan and execute a social media strategy.

Tools needed to plan and execute a social media strategy

Just like the architect needs many tools to plan and create a building plan, you need many tools to plan and execute an effective social media strategy. When it comes to social media marketing, there are many tools available that you can use to plan and execute your strategy, let's quickly talk about some of these tools.

Below are the tools you need to plan and execute an effective social media strategy

1. Social media calendar

Week 1	Sunday			Monday			...			Saturday		
Channel	Content	Image Link	Time	Content	Image Link	Time	Content	Image Link	Time	Content	Image Link	Time
Facebook												
Facebook												
Facebook												
Twitter												
Twitter												
Twitter												
Pinterest												
Pinterest												
Pinterest												
Instagram												
Instagram												
Instagram												
Google+												
Google+												
Google+												

Week 2	Sunday	Monday	...	Saturday						
Channel	Content	Image Link	Time	Content	Image	Time	...	Content	Image Link	Time
Facebook										
Facebook										
Facebook										

Just like your traditional calendar that helps you organize your daily activities, a social media calendar helps you to plan and execute your social media marketing strategies on a central calendar. This social media calendar makes it easy for you to see all your media contents, including posts and projects in one place.

There are many places where you could find a social media calendar for your own use. You can make use of apps like CoSchedule or use a spreadsheet-based calendar template. A quick Google search leads to various websites where you can download a spreadsheet-based social media calendar template like the one in the image above.

2. Curation tools

You need these tools to be able to find and share relevant content with your audience. There are so many free and paid curation tools out there that you can use. Let's quickly look at some content curation tools, both free and paid.

- **Newsletters**: Following the newsletters of popular websites and blogs that you would not want to miss their content is a good way to curate and share content that will interest your audience. Social media marketing thrives on the content you share with your audience. If you don't share incisive content, you may not get the results you need. So, follow the newsletters of websites and blogs that share content relevant to your market and audience. It is a free way of curating content.

- **Twitter Lists**: Twitter allows you to categorize and follow people differently from your normal list. This is a good way to curate content without having to go through so many junks. You can also create a pocket account to enable you to always save content directly from Twitter.

- Scoop.it: This is a paid tool; it has a similar interface with Pinterest. You start with topics that interest you and Scoop.it helps you generate articles relevant to the topic that you can view and share as well. Apart from showing you complementary topics that other Scoop.it users are following, the tool also sends you daily updates on the topics you follow to help keep you up to date with the most relevant topics to share. There is a free version that allows you to monitor only one topic.

Other curation tools include:

- TrapIt
- PublishThis
- Curata
- Sniply – costs between $29 - $299/month
- Storify
- Feedly

The particular content curator tool you use depends on your audience and the size of your campaign. The bottom-line is that content curation is an important part of social media marketing, as you always have to provide your audience with useful content.

When starting out, you may go with the free tools, but as you go higher in your marketing, consider getting the paid tools as they help you get more relevant content. Subscribe to the newsletters of websites and blogs that share content relevant to your market or audience.

3. Google Analytics

Google analytics helps you to track where your audience is coming from. When you create a post and include your referral link, you need to know the demographics that are clicking your referral link. The information can help you to further improve your products or services. And that's where Google Analytics comes to use. It is a free tool by Google; you may need to dedicate some time to learn how to use the tool to analyze your traffic

4. In-app Analytics

This is like Google analytics, but this time around, it is one built into the major social media platforms. These in-app analytics tools help you to track the performance of your campaigns and where your audience is coming from.

5. Buffer

Buffer is a great social media marketing tool that anyone serious about social media marketing must have. This tool allows you share your posts across several social media platforms at once. All you need do is to schedule when you want the tool to send out the posts to the various social media platforms, and you can do this from one central dashboard.

It has a Chrome extension that helps you send out a post to several social media platforms at the click of the mouse. If you don't know how to use the tool, visit their blog and read up and how to get started with the tool.

6. Bit.ly

Bit.ly is a link shortening tool. Not only does the tool allow you to shorten your links before attaching them to your posts, but it also allows you to track activities on the shortened link. Activities here include the number of people that clicked the link, the location of the people that clicked, the devices that they used to access the link, and so on.

There is a reason why you need this particular tool; shortened links are 80% more likely to get clicks than longer links. Links shortened using bit.ly often look like this, bit.ly/Po980yt.

7. Animoto

You can use this tool to create animated videos, and it is particularly useful when you are posting on Instagram, Snapchat or any of the other visual-based channels. You can add text overlays on your videos to instruct the viewer on what to do.

8. Grum

Instagram is a mobile-based platform, so you are expected to post content from your mobile device. But a tool like Grum allows you to post from your desktop. With Grum, you can do the following from a single dashboard on your Pc:

- Process and edit photos, including cropping images
- You can switch between your different accounts without signing out from any of them

- Prepare posts and schedule them to be posted at a later time
- Post on Instagram from your desktop

the scheduling functionality that the tool offers helps you schedule your posts when it would command the highest level of engagement.

9. Venngage

This tool helps you to create nice looking infographics. You can make use of existing charts and visuals from their library to create amazing infographics or tweak one of their many existing templates.

10. Viral Content Bee

This tool helps you to get others to share your content automatically

11. Facebook Messenger

You must engage your audience if you want to run a successful social media marketing and Facebook messenger is a hands-on tool for communicating with your audience in real time.

12. Brand24

This tool helps you sniff around the social media space and alerts you anytime your brand is mentioned. It is a great for knowing what others are saying about your brand and to respond accordingly.

13. Rival IQ

This tool helps you track all your engagement metrics from a single dashboard. The tool also helps you to compare the performance of your social media content with that of your competitors that you specify. This way, you know how to scale your content.

14. Buzzsumo

This is a useful social media marketing tool; it helps you to know what's trending on the social media space so that you can curate the most relevant contents for your audience.

The above are the major tools you need to plan and execute an effective social media strategy. Let's go ahead to look at how to create and execute a social media strategy in three simple steps.

Chapter Three: How to plan and execute a social media strategy

Choose your social networks

The different social media networks serve different purposes and depending on your market or audience; your campaign may thrive better on one network than the other. You have to look at your market and audience and decide which of the networks you will be running your campaigns on. You can choose multiple networks. To find your perfect social network, what you need is to research your target audience and the networks they frequent the most. Below are ways to choose the perfect social network for your social media marketing:

1. Find your target audience

If you know your audience and the social media network they frequent the most, you will be able to create content that appeals to them. To determine your target audience, it is good that you look at available data.

The statistics below can help you greatly to find the right social network that will get you the best results on your social media marketing campaigns.

Facebook's most popular demographics include the following:

- 89% of active Facebook users are women
- 88% of Facebook user are people between the ages of 18-29
- 84% of Facebook users earn less than $30,000
- 82% of Facebook users have some college experience

What does the above statistics show?

If your product is for low-income earners, then you should prioritize Facebook marketing in your social media strategy. If your product appeals to women, then you should also prioritize Facebook marketing. In fact, from the above statistics, Facebook can pass off as most business's ideal network for executing social media marketing.

Let's look at the other social media networks and see the most popular demographics there.

Instagram's most popular demographics include the following:

- 38% of Instagram users are women
- Only 26% of Instagram users are men
- 58% of Instagram users are between the ages of 18 and 29
- 39% of Instagram users are urban-located
- 38% of Instagram users earn less than $30,000
- 37% of Instagram users have college experience

From the above statistics, it is not difficult to see that most Instagram users are women. Hence, if your product or service appeals more to women, then Instagram should be your social media of choice for running your marketing campaigns. There are other deductions you can make from the above statistics. Example, if your product is for low-income earners, then you should also prioritize Instagram.

Twitter's most popular demographics include the following:

- 29% of Twitter users are women
- 36% of Twitter users are between the ages of 18 to 29

- 26% of Twitter users are urban-located

- 28% of Twitter users earn between $50,000 - $74,999

- 29% percent of Twitter users have college experience or more

Let's look at LinkedIn's most popular demographics below:

- 31% of LinkedIn users are men

- 34% of LinkedIn users are between the ages of 18-29

- 34% of LinkedIn users are urban-located

- 45% of LinkedIn users earn $75,000 or more

- 50% of LinkedIn users have college experience

Let's look at Snapchat and other auto-delete app's most popular demographics below:

- 24% of users are men

- 56% of users are between the ages of 18-29

- 27% of users earn less than $50,000

- 27% percent of users have college experience.

You can use the above statistics to know which social media platform is best for your business. Although the above demographics can't give you the complete insight as to which social network is best, you can still draw few inferences from them. Before you conclude on which network is best for you, you have to look at your customers and what they want.

There are many tools you can use to determine who is already following you and who are already interacting with your channel. We talked about some of these in a later chapter of this book. You can use the tools to know your channel that your customers are interacting with the most.

For example, if you already have a blog, use Google Analytics tools to know the social network that your readers are coming from. There are other tools you can use to determine your highest trafficked social networks.

2. Research your competitor's social networks

After finding out your most trafficked social networks, the next step in choosing your most preferred social network for your social media marketing is to find the networks that your competitors have the largest following on.

You know that you and your competitors are in the same market, and the social media networks that they operate can give you an insight into which one is ideal for your own business too.

You can start your competitor's social network by picking and writing down the names of at competitors. Pick five of them at least look for their channels on social media networks. Search for on Instagram, Facebook, Twitter, Google+, etc. For each of them, write down the number of followers they have on each of the channels. That can give you a rough idea of the channel that is best for your business. For example, if four of your competitors have the highest following on Facebook and Twitter, it means that Facebook and Twitter should be your preferred social media network.

3. Choose your social media channels

Armed with the information above, you are set to choose your best social media channel. You now know the demographics that are most active on the different social media channels. And knowing your type of business, you should use the demographics to choose the right channel.

Using the demographics that are most active on the different social media channels may not be enough; hence, you need to research the channel that your competitors command the highest following on. Reconcile the two data and choose a social media channel for your social media marketing campaigns.

List at least five of your competitors and their social media pages. Note the channels that they have the highest following on. To choose the best channel, start by making a list of the social media channels that are a top priority on your list. Rank them according to the ones that are most relevant to your business, and you would have succeeded in choosing the best social media channel for your social media marketing campaigns.

At the beginning of the chapter, we said that you could develop a social media strategy in three easy steps;

1. Choose your social networks

2. Plan your content

3. Make your social media promotion plan

We have already talked about the first one; in the next chapter, we'll look at how to plan your content.

Chapter Four: How to plan your content

In the previous chapter, we talked about choosing your social networks. In this chapter, we'll look at the second step in developing a social media strategy – how to plan your content.

The content you share with your followers on social media is critical. If you don't share content that resonates with their interest, they are going to leave. This is why you really need to take your time to plan on the type of content you will be sharing with your followers. You can't just be sharing anything that gets to your mind, no, you have to share something that your followers will find interesting.

Below are ways you can plan the content you share with your followers.

1. Think about your topics of expertise

If you have been able to select the right channel for your social media marketing campaigns, it means that you have followers who are interested in what you do, so you need to plan the topics you share with them to be ones that interest them. If your business is about food, for instance, and you have done your homework well and chosen the right social network, it means that your followers are going to be people who like food. Now, within the topic, there are subtopics, like intercontinental dishes, wines, local dishes, etc. There must be some subtopics in the list that you are excellent at. Mark those and always center your contents around those topics. This is to say that within your niche, you have sub-niches, and you should choose and stick to the sub-niches that you are more knowledgeable in.

When you are curating content, make sure that the contents are in line with the topics you are knowledgeable in. If a curated content doesn't fall into the list of the subtopics that you are knowledgeable in, don't share it with your followers. The reason for this shouldn't be hard to guess – if you share a subtopic that you are not knowledgeable in, your followers may ask you a question that may throw you off balance.

In addition to sharing content that falls within the topics you are knowledgeable in, make sure that the content you are sharing fits your brand. If the content doesn't fit your brand, then you are only wasting your time. The bottom line is to share content that does these two things:

1. The content must fit your brand

2. The content must be worthy

A good way to find the subtopics that fit the two criteria above is to draw a list of the three subtopics you are comfortable talking about. Make sure the topics have some kind of intersection. Intersection here means that they should fit your brand and at the same be worthy of sharing with your followers.

2. Find content to curate

Okay, you now know the topics or subtopics you want to share with your followers, now, how do you find the contents that fall within these subtopics. You need to plan how to find content to curate.

When you are looking for content to share with your followers; the following are rules you need to observe:

1. The content has to provide value to your followers

2. The content must be coming from an authority: you don't want to share unreliable information with your followers. If you do, you will dent your reputation greatly.

3. The content has to be timely. If you share content that your followers don't find relevant for the time being, then you are doing something wrong.

Use the content curation tools we talked about earlier to curate relevant content to share with your followers. Follow the newsletter of many reputable websites and blogs that fall within the subtopics that you had compiled earlier. Curate useful content from these websites to share with your followers. Set up Twitter lists, use Scoop.it to curate content. Use the other content curation tools to curate and share relevant content with your followers. When you are using the content curation tools, just enter the subtopics you want to curate and get all the relevant content you need.

Plan your execution

You now know the contents to share with your followers, and you have found a way of curating the content to share, next, you need to plan your content execution. The execution you should be planning here should include how to get images to use for your posts, the themes for your post, and finally, you need to have a content curation strategy.

The following are ways to plan your content execution:

1. Plan you imagery

Posts that have visual contents convert the most on social media. This is the major reason why Instagram and the other visual-based social networks command the most engagements. The human brain processes images faster than text, so people are always drawn to visual contents. Whether you are creating content for Instagram or Facebook or Twitter, or any of the other networks, plan a way of creating imagery for your posts.

You may not be good at creating imagery, but that's not a big problem. There are many applications and software programs out there that you can use to create imagery for your posts. Some of these imagery creation tools are free while some are paid for tools. If you are a small business or a solopreneur who can't afford to use the paid tools, then you can easily opt for the free ones. The free ones are good too. For example, **Canva** is an excellent desktop and mobile application that you can use to create professional looking designs for your posts. Images created with Canva look as professional as possible and the best thing about the app is its drag and drop feature that allows you to create any professional design you want.

2. Plan your campaigns

Different topics make headlines at different times of the year. If you are a social media calendar, you should have campaigns. For example, sometime around Christmas, you should have campaigns that reflect the season. Sometime around February, you should have campaigns that reflect the season, and the list continues. Different times of the year need different campaigns to yield the most effective results, use your social media calendar to plan your campaigns. Make sure that the campaigns reflect the different seasons on a calendar and that the campaigns fit your brand too.

There are tools you can use to create campaigns that are centered around promotions, holidays, events, etc. One of such tools is BuzzSumo to generate campaign ideas and plan your social media campaigns. Once you have generated your campaigns, use your social media calendar to plan how you are going to execute the campaigns.

When you are ready to create and publish your campaign content, your social media calendar will help you create a relevant content that reflects the different seasons.

3. Plan your curated content

An effective social media strategy entails sharing content regularly all through the year. Now, finding relevant content to share might be a bit challenging. Creating your own content all of the time is even more challenging, and that's why you need to plan your curated content.

Plan the specific days you will be sharing curated content, and the days you will be sharing your own contents. Make sure that the curated content you are sharing fits your brand. If you are using any of the content curation tools, make sure that the topics you curate are those that you are knowledgeable in and that the topics also fits your brand.

Now, you have chosen the best social network, and you have planned your content execution, the next thing you need to put into consideration to make your social media strategy complete is to make your social media promotion plan.

Chapter Five: Make your social media promotion plan

This is the time you refer back to your social media calendar. It is this calendar that will help sure that everything happens when it is supposed.

To go ahead with your social media promotion plan, you need to define your social media marketing goals. People engage in social media marketing for various reasons, and your reason for social media marketing will determine your approach when it comes to the promotion plans you adopt.

So, to develop an effective social media promotion plan, you need to define your goals.

Define your goals

Below are the reasons why different people engage in social media marketing:

1. To grow their audience: a lot of businesses and brands are on social media because they want to grow their audience. In fact, the majority of businesses that do social media marketing have this particular goal in mind. The reason is not far-fetched; they understand that the more their audience, the more the number of sales they record.

2. Increase blog traffic: this is yet another reason businesses run social media marketing campaigns. After creating useful blogs, businesses often want more people to read these blog contents. They understand that having huge readership can translate to sales and that's why many businesses spend money to run social media marketing to increase traffic to their blog.

3. To get more email subscribers: businesses understand that the larger their email subscription, the more sales they stand to make. And that's why many businesses run social media marketing campaigns to get more subscribers to their email list.

4. To drive more sales: yes, every business wants to drive sales, and social media marketing is an effective tool for doing that.

To make an effective social media promotion plan, you have to define the goals you want to achieve and make sure that the strategies you are laying down align with your goals.

To get the best results, you need to write down what you want, and you have to be very specific about it. If you know what you want beforehand, you will be able to make plans towards executing it. For example, if you want 5,000 page views each month on your blog posts, write it down. Being specific about the particular things you want will help you to always have the big picture in mind and to always strive towards it. With the big picture clearly written down, you will always go back to it to see your level of progress.

The bottom line is that you should define measurable goals for your social media marketing and map out ways of reaching such goals. You have to define your goals, have a big picture of the goals, and also be specific on how you want to achieve the goals. You need to understand that you don't really have goals until you have goals. Forgive my play on words; I was only trying to say that you can't make serious plans if you don't have goals. It is the goals that you set that give you a sense of direction, and once you have a sense of direction, it becomes way easier for you to get to your destination.

Once you have defined your goals, painted the big picture and listed the specifics on how you want to achieve your goals, next is for you to make plans on how often you will share content every day.

Plan how often you will share content every day

You will lose your followers if you are not consistent with your posts. The best way to grow your following and to maintain your existing following is to keep sharing content consistently.

Now, the hard question is, *"how often should you post on social media?"* The guide below will help get you on the right track on how often you need to post every day. With the guide, you no longer have to think about how often to post on social media while still getting all the benefits of increased awareness, engagement, shares, and traffic.

How often should you post on the different social networks?

On Facebook

You should endeavor to post at least once every day on Facebook. Posting to Facebook no more than once a day is best, or you will start to feel spammy. Depending on your audience, you should always post your content between 1:00 pm – 4 pm of the local time of your most active followers. For instance, if your audience is predominantly people from North America, then you should always post between 1:00 pm – 4:00 pm EST. Figure the time zone of your most active followers. You want to engage your followers with your post, and there is no better way to engage them than posting within the time frame that they are most active.

We have said that it is best for you to post once daily on Facebook, but if you must post more than once, let it not be more than two posts per day. You can curate and share a post every other day.

On Twitter

Since tweets are always shorter, you can post 15 tweets per day. Though you can make as low as one tweet per day and as high as 51 tweets per day, the recommended number of tweets for the best results is 15 per day.

When posting your tweets, make sure that you space them accordingly. Most retweets happen within an hour after tweeting, so a higher daily frequency is best.

Depending on the local time of your most active followers, your first tweet for any day should be made around 2:00 am. The second should follow around 3:00 am. Give some hours gap and start tweeting again between 6:00 am to 6:00 pm giving an hour gap between your tweets. Stop at 6:00 pm and resume again at 9 pm, and make sure that you have stopped tweeting at 10:00 pm each day.

Apart from tweeting your own content, you can also retweet or curate tweets every day. You can curate or retweet about seven tweets a day.

On Pinterest

The number of pins you should be posting daily on Pinterest is 11. Although you can go as low as 3 and as high as 30, 11 is the recommended number. You will see the best results with 11-30 pins per day when spread out throughout the day.

Your first pin for each day should be made around 2:00 am of the local time of your most active audience and pin again around 4:00 am. Resume pinning by 1:00 pm and continue till 4 pm when you stop to resume at 8:00 pm. At 11:00 pm each day, you should have stopped pinning for the day.

A good suggestion is to share 80% of your pins from other sources than your own blog, which would be about 9 pins out of your 11. For each day, repin or curate at least five pieces of content from others.

On LinkedIn

The recommended number of posts that you should make each day on LinkedIn is one. There are days you can decide not to make posts, and that's fine. Once a day should be the most you post on LinkedIn.

You should always post between 10:00 am and 11:00 am. You can curate or reshare a post every other day.

On Google+

The recommended number of posts you should always make on Google+ is 2. You can go as high as 3 and as low as 0, 2 is the recommended daily number. Share on Google+ a minimum of three times a week while 10 times per week should be your maximum. Curate or reshare one post every other day.

Your post for each should be made between 9:00 am and 11:00 am. While your second post for each day should be made between 12:00 pm and 1:00 pm.

On Instagram

The recommended number of posts you are to make on Instagram each day is around 1 to 2. You can go as high as 3 and as low as 1, 2 is the average and the recommended. Major brands share on Instagram on average 2 posts a day, but not more.

Your first post should be made between 8:00 am and 9:00 am. While your second post should be made around 2:00 am. Curate posts only when necessary and beneficial to your audience.

Make sure you set up a publishing plan that can help you share a specific piece of content the best way possible. This plan should capture how often you repost content that you had posted earlier.

If you are wondering if you can repost a post you had shared earlier, then you should think no more, as it is right to share a content you have shared before. Many times, not all your followers will see the content you shared, so the best way to make sure that everyone views your posts is to adopt a reposting plan that is reasonable. Remember that no one is comfortable with spam, so when reposting content, you have to observe the rules below:

- You can repost a tweet same day that you made the original tweet. You can repost the tweet a day after the original post; you can also repost a week, a month after the original post. The reason is simple to guess; twitter feeds change as fast as possible, and your audience may not always get to see the original post when you made them. And since tweets are relatively concise, your audience can always absorb it without feeling that you are spamming.

- You should only repost a Facebook post a month after the original post. Reposting a Facebook post earlier than a month after the original post date can constitute spam.

- You can repost a Google+ a week and a month after the original post

- You can repost a LinkedIn post a day after the original post.

- You can re-pin a post a day and a month after the original post on Pinterest.

When reposting an earlier post, just follow the rules above, so your audience doesn't see your posts as spam. Twitter's newsfeed cycle tweets frequently and your audience may not get to see a tweet when you made it, so it is nice that you repost your tweet several times after the original tweet.

Below is a summary of the posting frequency that we have talked about above

- Make one post on Facebook daily and curate one every other day
- Make one post on LinkedIn a day, and curate one every other day
- Make 15 tweets a day on twitter, and curate seven tweets every other day
- Make 3 posts per day on Pinterest and curate one post every other day
- Pin 11 pins a day on Pinterest and repin at least five pins per day

- Make 1-2 posts on Instagram every day and curate one a day.

Now, that you have the best posting frequency for each of the social networks, let's look at what time is best to post.

When is the best time to post?

Many times, people ask, *"when is the best time to post on social media?"* To answer that question, we've compiled the best time and days to reach your audience on Facebook, Twitter, Linked, Pinterest, Instagram, and Google+.

The best time to post depends on the location of your audience. We hinted earlier that your audience is what determines the best time for you to post. For example, if your audience is predominantly US residents, then the Eastern or Central time zone would be the best time to base off your posts. As you know, 80% of the US population is in the Central and Eastern time zones.

The best times to post on each of the social media channels

On Facebook

Facebook posts command higher engagement on weekends, especially Saturday and Sunday. In fact, Facebook posts command up to 32% engagement on Saturdays and Sundays. Facebook posts command the least levels of engagement on weekdays, that is from Monday to Wednesday.

Best time to post on Facebook is 9:00 am, 1:00 pm, and 3:00 pm. Posting at 3 pm will get you the most clicks, while 1 pm will get you the most shares. On what kind of posts you should make on weekends to command higher engagement; you need to understand that people often seem happier on weekends, so funny or upbeat content will fit right into that happiness index.

Quick tip: Use Facebook analytics to track your data and see when your audience is online.

When is the best time to post on Twitter?

The best time to post on Twitter are 12 pm, 3 pm, and 5-6pm. The best day to post on Twitter is Wednesday.

Now, on the kinds of posts that command the highest engagement; B2B performs 16% better during business hours. B2C performs 17% better on weekends.

The best idea is to use Twitter analytics to track your own followers to find the best time to tweet. This doesn't just apply to Twitter, but it applies to all the social networks. Even though you could benefit from the general ideas on the best time to post, it is best that you use the in-app analytics of the different channels to determine which time of the day that your post command the highest engagements.

Best time to post on LinkedIn

LinkedIn posts command the highest levels of engagement on weekdays, that is between Tuesdays and Thursdays. The best time to post on LinkedIn are 7-8am, 12 pm, and 5-6pm. Business people are most likely to read LinkedIn in the morning like the newspaper. While LinkedIn is more professional, the best time to post is still before and after work.

Best times to pin on Pinterest

The best days to post on Pinterest are Saturdays and Sundays. And the subjects that command the highest levels of engagement on these two days are food and travel respectively. For Mondays to Fridays, the following command the highest levels of engagement, fitness, gadgets, quotes, outfits, and gifts respectively.

The best time to post on Pinterest is 8-11pm, especially on Saturdays. The worst time on Pinterest is during work hours. When posting on Pinterest, make sure to include a call to action. 80% of people that see your content during the peak times won't interact otherwise.

Best time to post on Instagram

The best days to post on Instagram if you want to command a high level of engagement are Mondays and Thursdays. Sundays command the lowest levels of engagement. The best time to post is between 8-9am. Avoid posting at 3-4pm. Posting a video on Instagram at 9 pm gets 34% more interactions. To get the highest levels of engagement, post content more during off-work hours than during the work hours.

Best days and time to post on Google+

Avoid posting during early mornings or late evenings on Google+. The best time to post is between 9-11am, especially on Wednesdays. 90% of the people on Google+ are just lurkers and will not interact with your content.

The above about summarizes the best time and days to post on different social networks. To get the most results, you have to post on more networks; more networks equals more levels of engagement.

Utilize more than one network

Even though there may just be a single network that is best suited for your brand, you don't have to ignore the other channels. Every other channel has their own purpose, but you will still benefit from posting on all the networks.

For example, Sunday is the day that Facebook posts command the highest engagement; if you are posting only on Facebook, it means that you will record low social media activity on the other days of the week. Again, LinkedIn posts command the highest level of engagement on Tuesdays, so, if you are posting on LinkedIn alone, your social media channels would only record high level of activity on Tuesdays. However, if you are consistent on all the channels, you will always maintain a high level of activity every day of the week. And you know that consistency is essential when it comes to social media marketing.

Twitter is very good regarding social media marketing because Twitter is effective each day of the week, but remember to consider your audience.

Let's look at the various social media channels and their strong points

1. Facebook is broadly used on mobile and desktop, at work and home. It really depends on the audience as far as who and how it is used

2. Twitter is a hard nut to crack, and definitely audience-dependent, like Facebook. It is often treated like an RSS feed,

and something to read during downtimes like commutes, breaks, and so on.

3. Pinterest users seem to make network activity an evening sport, much like sitting down to a TV in the evening during their free time.

4. Google+ also targets work professionals with the average users interacting in the early morning.

5. Instagram users are on a platform meant for mobile, and that means they tend to use the network all the time, anytime.

6. LinkedIn is for professionals, and they tend to use it around work hours.

The bottom line is that you should stay consistent with the times you are posting. Use a general approach to several resources. Find the ones that work best for your audience.

Plan your promoted content

You can't run a successful social media marketing without promoting your posts. Don't confuse promoted post and social media ads; they are two different things. Promoted posts are your regular posts or what they call organic posts that you have paid to get across to as many people as possible. While social media ads are as they sound, paid advertisement content.

When you want to set up a promoted post, many social media channels like Pinterest, LinkedIn, Instagram, Facebook give you a chance to choose the demographics to target; you are also allowed to set your budget, the location you want to target, etc.

Among the things you are allowed to set are:

1. Location of your audience: If your audience or customers are from a specific region, you target them when setting up your promoted post on the different social media channels. This way, only the people you want to see your post gets to see it.

2. Audience targeting: In addition to setting the location of your audience, you can also set who you would like to reach.

3. Budget limit: Every social media platform allows you to set a maximum amount you are willing to spend daily promoting your posts.

There are many other things you can set when you want to promote your content on social media. Now, when you want to record your content promotion plans on your social media calendar, there are three steps you need to take:

1. Decide your end goal

Earlier, we noted that social media marketing could be used to achieve different purposes. When you want to promote your content on social media, the first step is to determine the purpose you want to achieve with the promoted post. Remember the goals you set out earlier, and think about how promoting your post is going to help you achieve those goals.

On your document, you can lay out the posts you want to promote and the goals you want to achieve with the promotion.

Date Running	Channel	Budget	Target Audience	Goal of Boosted Post	Results
1 Dec - 25 Dec	Facebook			Increase Page Views	

2. Set your target audience

After you have determined the goal you want to achieve promoting your posts, next is to set your audience. What target audience do you want to see your posts? If you don't target the right audience, then you will be simply wasting money and efforts promoting your posts. For instance, if you have a platform that connects people of opposite sex and you have written a post on *"how to behave well on a first date"* meant to promote your service, your target audience are single people who are looking to mingle. If you go ahead and target married people, then you won't see results.

Date Running	Channel	Budget	Target Audience	Goal of Boosted Post	Results
1 Dec - 25 Dec	Facebook		Age 18- 35	Increase Page Views	

3. Set your budget

The next step in promoting your post is to set your budget for the overall promotion. You can also set the amount you are willing to pay daily for post promotion. For many networks, the more the number of people you want to reach with your post, the more money you pay.

Date Running	Channel	Budget	Target Audience	Goal of Boosted Post	Results
1 Dec - 25 Dec	Facebook	$20 Per Day	Age 18- 35	Increase Page Views	

Record your daily results in your document

4. Evaluate your results

Date Running	Channel	Budget	Target Audience	Goal of Boosted Post	Results
1 Dec - 25 Dec	Facebook	$20 Per Day	Age 18- 35	Increase Page Views	Incr. Page Views by 25%

After running a post promotion, record your results and compare the result you get with the goals you set out initially. If your goals had been to get more visitors to your website, you have to check if you have achieved the result. If the content promotion helped you achieve your aims, consider rerunning the promotion, otherwise, change your metric like the audience, location, etc., and continue to run the promotion until you have the right combination of metrics that yield the best results.

Chapter Six: How to compose a post that converts

This applies to when you are posting your content on social media. Whether you are posting content on your newsfeed or using pay per click (PPC) ads to get your content to your audience, make sure that you use the social media rule of thirds. I'll explain what the social media rule of thirds is shortly.

Many times, it is tempting for businesses to share content containing only promotional messages, neglecting authentic engagement. In fact, it comes naturally to you just to share your branded promotional messages ignoring to take to heart the needs of your followers. That's why the social media rule of thirds is essential.

What is social media rule of thirds? The rule states the following,

- One-third of your posts should be promotional

- One-third of your posts should provide value to your fans

- One-third of your posts should engage fans in some way.

Let's look at these rules one at a time.

1. Share promotional content: Yes, it is important to promote your brand, talk about your past events, your present events and future events. Just the normal promotional content. This is not where the problem lies because people rarely break this particular rule, it is the other two rules that we see people break all of the time.

2. Share content that provides value to your audience: Remember that you are trying to build a loyal fan base and part of your duty should be to provide these your fans with valuable content. What are the things that could pass as valuable content? It could be by curating other useful content from other sources. Curate and share useful content with your audience every other day. This singular act can go a long way in giving your brand huge exposure. Talking about general industry news can also be a nice way for you to demonstrate your kick-ass industry knowledge, and help establish your brand's authority.

Remember not to over-do it though, and don't go promoting old news. Study your audience and know what they would enjoy reading, what would increase your social media reach, and entwine it in-between your own content. After all, you won't want to appear like you've done nothing yourself now, do you?

Below are some value adding sharing prospects to consider:

- News and important industry updates

- Articles, links, and stories from key industry leaders/influencers

- Trending industry hashtags and keywords

- Good reviews and mentions of you, of course! Although this may slightly overlap with self-promotion, technically it wasn't you, so, it is still all good.

Furthermore, never claim content that is not yours. If you share any content, don't forget to give credit to the original owner. Always offer your perspective on the topic at hand and encourage your fans to do the same – it's all about getting that social media ball rolling!

3. Engage your fans in some way

A third of your posts on social media should focus on building the personal side of your brand. Engaging your fans with your posts portrays the human side of you. Your fans are living beings, and they will be happy to know that they are dealing with humans too and not some robots. So, with regards to this, here are some tips on how you can humanize your social media content:

- Get involved with commenting, likes, and replying the messages of your fans. Try as much as possible to reply to every comment directed at you.

- Tailor your language and tone of voice to your audience and circumstance – if you are sharing a joke, then it's okay to #LOL about it.

- Never keep your audience hanging. Reply to comments directed at you and direct messages as quickly as possible.

- No matter how busy you may be, always find time to interact often. It helps you build relationship

Following these rules will help you always to reel out balanced messages and content to your audience, and hence, increase the number of your loyal followers.

Final words

Running an effective social media marketing starts with developing an effective social media strategy. A social media strategy is to social media marketing what a building plan is to a house. It is what defines all the coordinated activities you have to go through to achieve results.

You can develop a social media strategy in three steps; define your goals, choose your social networks, and plan your content. Once you plan the three steps well, what you get is social media marketing that yields results.

As a reminder, below are things you must integrate into your social media marketing campaigns.

1. Action gate: Don't just reel content out there and expect users to know what to do. It is your job to tell them what you want them to do. Do you want them to enter contests, provide reviews, take surveys, or join mailing lists? Communicate it to them with your content.

2. Provide incentives: People will more readily leave you with their information if they have something to gain. Incentives like free giveaways, discounts, and special price offers will entice people any day, anytime to leave you with their information.

3. Ensure you engage users: Reply to comments and address critique quickly and reinforce positive interactions with personal attention.

4. Don't focus on one medium: Even though your campaign could thrive better on one medium than the other, you still do not have to ignore the others. For instance, if your campaigns have pictorial elements that will obviously thrive better on Instagram and Pinterest, there could still be a place for the campaign on Twitter and Facebook.

5. Monitor your campaign: Use the tools I talked about somewhere up there to monitor your campaign to see how it's performing. If your campaign is doing well, you improve on your strategies, and if it's not, you re-strategize.

1. Choose Your Social Networks

First step is to choose the social networks that are best suited for your business

Research the networks that receive highest from the different demographics

Use Google analytics to find the networks that receive the highest traffic

Network	Traffic Metric
Instagram	
Facebook	
Twitter	
LinkedIn	
Pinterest	
Google+	

Research the networks that your competitors have more following

You and your competitors have the same audience, so research their audience

Network	1st Competitor	2nd Competitor	3rd Competitor	4th Competitor
Twitter				
Instagram				
Facebook				

Pinterest				
Google+				

List your social media platforms

Develop a list of all the social networks where you are active.

Social media platform 1:

Your business username on the platform:

Social media platform 2:

Your business username on the platform:

.

.

.

Social media platform n:

Your business username on the platform:

2. Plan The Content You'll Share

If you are not consistent in sharing content on social media, you will lose your followers

What are the topics you are knowledgeable in?

List your topics and subtopics of expertise

Topic 1:

Subtopic 1:

Topic 2:

Subtopic 2:

.

.

Topic n:

Subtopic n:

What kind of posts can you create?

Look at your abilities and determine the kinds of content you can create

Imagery:

List your available tools for this:

Video

List your available tools for this:

Writing

List your available tools for this:

Curated Content

List your content curation tools:

Campaigns

List your available tools for this:

How Will You Participate In The Conversation?

Plan the times when you will monitor and listen. Block these times out on your appointment calendar and set up notifications to remind you to check in on your social networks.

Monday	Tuesday	Wednesday	Thursday	Friday	Saturday	Sunday

3. Make Your Social Media Promotion Plan

Now that you know what networks you'll be on—and the ways you'll be using them—it's time to make the plan.

Define Your Goals

What is it you want to accomplish with social media?

Define the #1 reason you're using social media: {Reason}

How will you measure that goal? {Metric}

How much of that metric do you want to receive weekly/monthly: {Number per time frame}

How will you measure that metric? {Tool(s) you'll use to measure your goal}

How often will you measure? {Time/day/frequency when you'll measure}

Plan How Often You Will Share Every Day

Knowing your daily sharing frequency will help you understand how much content to produce and variety to add to your social sharing.

Facebook: {Number per time frame}

Twitter: {Number per time frame}

LinkedIn: {Number per time frame}

Pinterest: {Number per time frame}

Google+: {Number per time frame}

Instagram; {Number per time frame}

Outline Your Content Sharing Plan

Now analyze how many times you will share a specific piece of content like a blog post, for example. This will be your template for sharing a single project via social media.

When	Facebook	Twitter	LinkedIn	Pinterest	Google+	Instagram
On publish						
Day after						
3 days after						

Week after						
Month after						
Custom						

Plan Your Budget

Going into any expenditure without knowing where the budget line is drawn is a super bad idea.

How much money can you allocate each month to paid social media promotion? {Number}

On which social networks will you experiment with paid promotion? {Social network names}

Keep Track of Your Boosted Posts

Date Running	Channel	Budget	Target Audience	Goal of Boosted Post	Results
1 Dec - 25 Dec	Facebook	$20 Per Day	Age 18- 35	Increase Page Views	Incr. Page Views by 25%

www.ingramcontent.com/pod-product-compliance
Lightning Source LLC
LaVergne TN
LVHW052311060326
832902LV00021B/3826